Nehru for Children

By
M. Chalapathi Rau

Children's Book Trust, New Delhi

Photographs courtesy: Nehru Memorial Museum and Library, New Delhi

© by CBT 1967
Reprinted 1971, 1973, 1976, 1979, 1982, 1985, 1987, 1988, 1989,
1992, 1996, 1997, 1999, 2001, 2003, 2004, 2005, 2008.
Revised edition 2012
Reprinted 2014

ISBN 81-7011-035-1

Published by Children's Book Trust, Nehru House, 4 Bahadur Shah
Zafar Marg, New Delhi-110002 and printed at its Indraprastha Press.
Ph: 23316970-74 Fax: 23721090 e-mail: cbtnd@cbtnd.com
Website: www.childrensbooktrust.com

राष्ट्रपति भवन, नई दिल्ली—4
RASHTRAPATI BHAVAN
NEW DELHI-4
November 2, 1967

"If you were with me," Jawaharlal Nehru writes in one of his letters to the children of India, "I would love to talk to you about this beautiful world of ours, about flowers and trees and birds and animals and stars and mountains and glaciers and all the other wonderful things that surround us... You must have read many fairy tales and stories of long ago. But the world itself is the greatest fairy tale and story of adventure that has been written. Only we must have eyes to see and ears to hear and a mind that opens out to the life and beauty of the world."

Jawaharlal Nehru is no longer there to talk to children: his message has to be carried to them so that they open out their minds to life and beauty.

The life of anyone who has attained eminence in this world should convince us of the value of awareness, responsiveness, and courage. I trust that the young readers of this book will discover what remarkable effect the presence of these qualities had on Jawaharlal Nehru's life, and how they became the secret of his greatness.

He was aware of the beauty to be enjoyed and the

ugliness to be removed. He felt as if all that was happening in the world was happening to him and it was his personal concern to see that the right thing was done. He had the courage to say and to do what he believed was right. But even when he was struggling against evil, against British rule in India or domination of one country by another anywhere in the world, he was anxious to see that the beautiful was not destroyed in the conflict.

He loved children and flowers and birds, but his love of friendship and peace among men and nations was deeper still, because that was for him the most beautiful and desirable of all things. It was to this that he dedicated all his thought and energy, and he did it with a smile that has become a part of our history.

I must congratulate the Children's Book Trust on persuading Chalapathi Rau to write this book to introduce Nehru to the children of India he so dearly loved and who returned his love in such simple but touching manner. Few men could have done this better than Chalapathi Rau who not only knew Nehru intimately, but also understood him deeply.

(DR. ZAKIR HUSAIN)
President of India

1   Childhood

Jawaharlal Nehru was one of the greatest men the world has known. He was brave, kind and generous. In his life of seventy-five years, he always worked hard and never knew fear. He was born rich, but he lived like an ordinary man. For a long time he fought for the freedom of the country, by the side of Mahatma Gandhi and other leaders. After the country attained freedom, he was its first Prime Minister, for seventeen long years.

He worked to make India happy and prosperous. He worked for the unity of the people belonging to different races, religions, and communities, for peace in the world, and for an understanding between nations. He worked till the last; he died working. Throughout his life he loved the people greatly, and they too loved him immensely. He loved children especially, and they loved him and called him 'Chacha' (Uncle) Nehru. The story of his life is one of noble words and noble deeds.

Jawaharlal was born on November 14, 1889, in Allahabad. The day is celebrated by the people as Children's Day. His father was Motilal Nehru, a well-

Jawaharlal with his parents

known and prosperous lawyer, and his mother was Swarup Rani, a pretty, sweet and noble woman with a doll-like face. The Nehrus were Brahmins who had come from Kashmir, the most loveliest part of India and one of the most beautiful places in the world. They lived in Delhi first and then moved to Agra. Motilal was born there on May 6, 1861.

Motilal's father, Gangadhar Nehru, was the Kotwal, the chief police official of Delhi. He died before Motilal was born. His elder brothers, Bansidhar Nehru and Nandalal Nehru, brought up Motilal. Nandalal practised as a lawyer first in Agra and then in Allahabad. Motilal attended the Government High School in Kanpur and later studied at the Muir Central College in Allahabad.

Motilal was to become a famous leader. He was handsome, brilliant, and of a strong will. In the B.A. examination he thought he had not done well in the first paper and so he did not appear for the second. His professor rebuked him because he had secured good marks in the first paper. Motilal decided to be a lawyer, like his brother. He stood first in the examination for High Court lawyers. After sometime, he settled down in Allahabad to practise at the High Court.

Allahabad is a historic city. It stands at the meeting place of three rivers, the Ganga, the Yamuna, and the Saraswati which for a long time has only flowed underground. The meeting of the three rivers is called Sangam and the place is considered very holy. Pilgrims from all over India come here to bathe in these waters. Allahabad was also, for many years, the capital of the United Provinces of Agra and Avadh, and has had a High Court where famous lawyers have practised and lived rich lives. It is a seat of learning. Several notable men have lived here at one time or another.

Jawaharlal had a good family background, a rich and famous father, and a loving mother. Motilal lived first in the Chowk, an old part of the city, then moved to the Civil Lines, where mostly Europeans lived; and in 1900, when Jawaharlal was ten, he purchased a palatial house called Anand Bhawan (Abode of Happiness). Anand Bhawan had

Anand Bhawan

many rooms, large lawns, and a swimming pool. Many famous men and women from near and distant parts of India went there and stayed with the Nehrus.

Motilal was a great host and had a very English lifestyle; he was a good talker knew several languages, and was full of wit and humour. Jawaharlal was the only son of the family and the only child for many years. Hence he was the object of much love. His sister, Swarup, who is now famous and well-known as Vijayalakshmi Pandit, was born in 1900, and a second sister, Krishna, was born in 1907. With Swarup much younger than him and Krishna not yet born, Jawaharlal was a lonely boy.

Motilal visited Europe several times and bought for him many things from there, such as cycles and motor cars. After his first visit in 1899, he was expelled from his community because he would not perform the purification ceremony. Jawaharlal was brought up like an English boy. He rode a tricycle or a small pony.

Learned Brahmins were engaged to teach him Hindi and Sanskrit, but with little success. He was sent to St. Mary's Convent School. After six months he was removed from the school and was then coached at home by an English tutor, Ferdinand Brooks, a young man in his twenties. Under the guidance of Brooks, Jawaharlal read novels, romances and books on religion and science.

He liked to read books by Scott, Thackeray, Dickens, Kipling, Lewis Carroll and H.G. Wells. He specialy enjoyed books like *Alice in Wonderland* by Lewis Carroll,

Kim by Kipling, *The Prisoner of Zenda* by Anthony Hope, and *Three Men in a Boat* by Jerome K. Jerome. Brooks taught him chemistry also. Jawaharlal did experiments in a crude laboratory or played about with a magnet and the geometry box. He developed a taste for riding and became a good horseman. He was a good swimmer though he played some cricket and tennis too.

Annie Besant, an Irish woman who had made India her home, was a famous leader at this time and she was a great orator. Jawaharlal came under her spell and joined the Theosophical Society founded by her. The society was interested in religious thought and worked earnestly to make known India's past. But Jawaharlal soon became tired of Theosophy. Though he loved to read and ponder over his thoughts, he loved action and men of action more. His father, Motilal, was himself a man of action. Jawaharlal stood in awe of his magnificent father. Like him, Jawaharlal was influenced by Mogul culture and western ideas. He was at ease in the English language. While he was fond of the English people he did not like Englishmen to rule over Indians.

Japan and Russia were fighting each other at that time. The Japanese victories stirred Jawaharlal. He waited for fresh news daily, and he read books about Japan. He thought of Asian freedom and Indian freedom. He dreamt of doing brave deeds, how he would, sword in hand, fight for India and help her to be free.

Jawaharlal was steadily growing up and was now fourteen. There were changes in the family household. Motilal's brothers had died and Motilal had brought up his brothers' children. These elder cousins of Jawaharlal were now leaving their home and the lonely boy was lonelier than ever.

2   Harrow and Cambridge

Motilal wanted Jawaharlal to be educated in England. In May 1905, when Jawaharlal was fifteen, his family, that is, his father, mother, his baby sister, and himself, set sail for England.

Jawaharlal was admitted to the famous public school at Harrow. He was fortunate to find a vacancy there for he was slightly above the usual age for entry into the school. The parting from the family was hard. Motilal, writing a farewell letter before leaving Europe, referred to him as their 'dearest treasure'. Jawaharlal was for the first time among strangers and for a while he felt lonely and homesick. Then he began to take part in school activities, and work and play kept him busy. But he was conscious of the fact that he was not one of them, and so he kept to himself. He had his share in the games, though he did not do too well in them. But he was no shirker.

He was in a low form to begin with, because of his little knowledge of Latin, but he soon rose higher. In general knowledge and in many subjects he was ahead of other boys. His interests were wider and he read both books and newspapers more than the others did. He wrote to his father how dull most of the English boys were; they could talk about nothing but their games. Some of them, however, were bright, especially those in the upper forms.

At the end of 1905 there was a general election in England which was won by the Liberal Party. Early in 1906 the form-master asked the boys about the new government. To his surprise, Jawaharlal was the only boy who could give much information on the subject, including an almost complete list of the new ministers.

Jawaharlal was not immersed in politics alone. Those were the early days of flying and he was interested in its progress. The Wright brothers and others made their first flights and Jawaharlal was thrilled. He wrote to his father that soon he might be able to pay a weekend visit to India by air.

In 1906, in the track and field competition, he won the half mile race and was placed third in the mile event. He was awarded a prize for topping the examination list in his form during the third term in 1905 and again in the first term in 1906. Dr. Wood, the Headmaster of Harrow, was satisfied with him in every way and sent good reports to Motilal. Motilal was pleased.

Jawaharlal liked Harrow. He joined the Rifle Club and the Cadet Corps, yet he began to feel he was outgrowing Harrow. The university attracted him. During the years 1906 and 1907 the news from India disturbed him. There was little news in the papers he read in England, whatever he read made him feel that big events were happening in his home country, in the Bengal, Punjab and Maharashtra region. There was a boycott of British goods and a movement for swadeshi, or Indian-made goods. All this stirred his mind. But there was no one

As a cadet at Harrow

at Harrow to whom he could talk about it. It was only when, during the holidays, he met some cousins or friends that he could express his thoughts. In the summer of 1906 he went to India and spent three weeks with his parents in Mussoorie. Back in England, he wrote his comments on Indian politics to his father, and he wanted more and more information in return.

At this time Jawaharlal came to know the story of Italian freedom and unity. As a prize he was given a book by the British historian George Macaulay Trevelyan on Garibaldi, a great Italian hero. The book impressed him and he soon got the other books on Garibaldi and studied his heroic life. He thought that in India too there might be a strong

At Cambridge

movement for freedom, as there had been in Italy.

Harrow seemed a rather small place for these ideas and he wanted a wider sphere. His father agreed, and he left Harrow after only two years' stay. When the time came to part he felt unhappy, and tears came to his eyes. He had grown fond of the place.

At the beginning of October 1907, when he was approaching eighteen, Jawaharlal joined Trinity College. It is a famous college the University of Cambridge and has produced many Prime Ministers. He was happy to have joined such a prestigious college.

Jawaharlal had a great deal of freedom to do what he liked. He felt he was not a boy now but a grown-up. He wandered about the big courts and narrow streets of Cambridge. He was there for three years, three quiet years with little of disturbance in them. But the years were not wasted. He got to learn a lot.

Jawaharlal studied for the Natural Science Tripos (framework within which most of the science is taught in Cambridge). His subjects were chemistry, geology and botany. But his interests were wider. He met many people at Cambridge, or during the vacations in London, who talked about books and literature, history, politics, and economics. At first he knew little of these subjects but he read a few books and was soon able to fully comprehend them. He discussed even difficult authors and books. He came into contact with socialist ideas, and he came under the influence of Bernard Shaw and Bertrand Russell. Along with his friends, he considered himself very clever. At this time, people liked an easy life and pleasant experiences. Jawaharlal was attracted by the beautiful side of life. He too wanted to get the most out of life but not through vulgar display. There was much to be done and much to be seen. The problems of life were yet not so grave. It was the time before the First World War.

Jawaharlal's life was filled with work, games and entertainment. The political struggle in India stirred him. Meredith Townsend's book *Asia and Europe* influenced him greatly. India was full of unrest and trouble. The people were prepared to fight against foreign rule. He was glad his father had become very active in politics. They corresponded regularly. But Jawaharlal was critical of Motilal's moderate politics.

The Indians in Cambridge had a society called the Majlis, and there they held debates on political problems. But they discussed everything but the real issue. Jawaharlal attended the Majlis debates but hardly ever spoke there. He was shy and diffident. In the college debating society there was a rule that if a member did not speak for a whole term, he had to pay a fine. Jawaharlal often paid the fine. He was later to become one of the finest speakers of his time.

During Jawaharlal's time at Cambridge, some famous Indian leaders visited the Indian students and talked to them. The Indian students felt superior to the British students because they thought theirs was a vast culture and they could take a broader view of things. Among the Indian students of that time, some were to become well-known leaders, while some joined government service.

In 1908 Jawaharlal had a brief vacation in India. In 1909 Motilal went to Europe and Jawaharlal joined him. Father and son saw Count Zeppelin arrive in his new airship in Berlin; and they saw aviation feats in Paris.

Jawaharlal was twenty when he took his degree from Cambridge with second class honours in the Natural Science Tripos. It was 1910. For a little while there were suggestions that he should join the Indian Civil Service (I.C.S.). It was considered the highest service at that time and only bright students could sit for the examination. But the idea was dropped as he was underage. Besides, neither his father nor he was keen on it. Also, if he joined the I.C.S. he would be posted in various places distant from home. His father and mother wanted him near them after his long absence.

It was decided then that he join the Bar, like his father. Jawaharlal joined the Inner Temple, London. His law studies did not take up much time. He did a lot of general reading and he took an interest in socialist ideas and the Irish freedom movement. He could think much and discuss much. He got through the Bar examinations

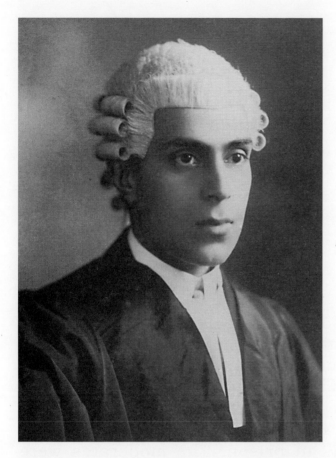

The young barrister

easily. In the summer of 1912 he became a barrister, and in the autumn he returned to India after a stay of over seven years in England. In these seven years he came home only twice, during his holidays.

Jawaharlal was a spendthrift. Motilal mildly remonstrated with him. Once Jawaharlal wanted to buy a motor car, but Motilal rejected the idea because he was afraid of accidents. However, Jawaharlal was very adventurous. Once he had the narrowest of escapes while plunging into a mountain torrent in Norway.

3   Homecoming

On his return home from England, Jawaharlal found India politically dull. The nationalist leaders were divided into extremists and moderates. The extremists were those who wanted strong action against the British. The moderates were those who believed in argument. The extremists at this time were without their leader, Tilak, for he was in prison. The moderates were cooperating with the British. The Congress, which was the organization of Indian nationalists, was at this time a moderate group.

Jawaharlal was a delegate to the Congress session at Bankipore, in Patna, in 1912. He found it was an upper class affair, with everyone speaking English. Most of the delegates wore morning coats and well-ironed trousers. It was like a social gathering, not a political meeting. It had little to do with the people. Jawaharlal was disappointed.

He joined the High Court. He took an interest in his work, but he slowly grew tired of the dull routine. Life was pleasant at first, but it soon lost its freshness. He often went to the Bar library and to the club, and the same people were to be found in both, talking about the same things, often about law and the law courts. Jawaharlal found his routine very unexciting.

Jawaharlal was dissatisfied with life. He liked the outings but did not take too kindly to the killings. Since law did not engage him fully, he started taking interest in hunting. Politics to him meant rebellion against foreign rule, but there was no scope for it then. He joined the Congress and worked hard when there was action. But there was not always action.

Gopal Krishna Gokhale, the great moderate leader, had founded the Servants of India Society in Pune in 1905. Its members were engaged in social and other service. They led simple lives and received only the bare means of livelihood. Jawaharlal was at first attracted to the society. But the policies of the organization were too moderate for him and he did not join it.

The First World War broke out in August 1914. The Germans and their allies were fighting against the British and their allies. India had no interest in the war but she was brought into it without her consent. She was kept under tight control by the British. There were loud declarations of loyalty from some people but among most people there was no love for the British, who were the rulers. There was also no love for Germany. Jawaharlal's sympathies were with France, who was on the side of the British and was attacked by the Germans.

The Indian people helped the British but they also wanted freedom from British rule. Slowly, political life grew again. Bal Gangadhar Tilak came out of Mandalay prison in Burma (now Myanmar) and he helped found the All India Home Rule League in 1916–18 with Annie Besant and other fellow nationalists to demand freedom from British rule. Stirring speeches were made. The sessions of the Congress and of the Muslim League, which was an organization of the Muslims, became exciting. The atmosphere became tense. Annie Besant was interned and this angered even the moderates.

Motilal was at first a moderate. Other moderate leaders resigned from Annie Besant's Home Rule League, but he remained in it. He was by nature rebellious and he gradually became a strong nationalist. Motilal and Jawaharlal influenced each other. Motilal believed in argument; Jawaharlal was youthful and impulsive. Motilal had an aristocrat's ways; Jawaharlal wanted to adopt the ways of the people. They first came under the influence of Annie Besant. And when she turned a moderate, they came under the influence of Gandhi.

Jawaharlal was gradually drawn into political activities. He was shy of speaking in public. He felt that public speeches should not be in English and he did not know if he could speak at length in Hindi.

It was in 1915 that he made his first public speech in Allahabad. It was at a meeting held to protest against a new law. He spoke briefly but in English. And as soon as the meeting was over, Tej Bahadur Sapru, a leading moderate leader, embraced and kissed his in public forehead.

There were arguments between moderates and extremists and there were arguments between Motilal and Jawaharlal. Sometimes the arguments became heated. Motilal was too obstinate to change easily. He took time for each step. But once he felt strongly and thought it was right, he took the step and there was no going back for him.

It was during the Lucknow Congress in 1916 that

Jawaharlal first met Gandhi. Gandhi had become a legend by then. But he was yet distant. Soon Motilal and Jawaharlal were to know him well and work with him closely.

Annie Besant

Bal Gangadhar Tilak

Gopal Krishna Gokhale

4   Kamala

Jawaharlal was married on Basant Panchami day on February 8, 1916 in Delhi. The bride was Kamala Kaul, a pretty young woman of 16 years. It was a happy marriage. Jawaharlal took Kamala to Kashmir. She was shy and tender, and Jawaharlal liked to tell her what he knew of the world and of the spirit of freedom which was sweeping the country. A daughter was born to them on November 19, 1917. She was named Indira Priyadarshini.

Kamala soon showed that she was a brave woman of strong will. She joined Jawaharlal and other members of the family in the freedom struggle. She also went to prison several times and had her share of suffering. When she was out of prison she organized volunteers and led protests. Jawaharlal's mother also joined the struggle. Even at 12, little Indira did her share of work by organizing a group of children, called the Monkey Brigade, to run errands for Congress prisoners.

Kamala had a little schooling but she had no formal education. She was a simple young woman, with a girlish look. But her eyes had depth and fire. She was a traditional woman who had little difficulty in adapting to modern ways of life. A Kashmiri girl, Kamala was sensitive and proud. She was reserved in front of some people, but she was gay and frank with those she knew and liked. She had strong likes and dislikes. She was very sincere, too.

Jawaharlal was busy as a nationalist worker and leader and for long periods he almost forgot Kamala. He could not give her his company, for he was living in a world of his own. Yet he did not forget her entirely. He went back to her again and again. She gave him comfort and strength and comradeship. He sometimes felt that he was taking much from her and not giving enough back. She never sought his help. She played her own part in the national struggle and was not anybody's shadow. Jawaharlal was in prison often and she was left to herself. And she too went to prison.

In the early months of 1930, Jawaharlal and Kamala worked closely together. This was a new delight to them. But there was national unrest again, and the Salt Satyagraha began. Jawaharlal was in prison once more.

The bride and bridegroom

Then a remarkable thing happened. The men were in prison but the women came to the forefront and took charge of the struggle. This time they played their part in large numbers. These women belonged to all classes. Rich women, peasant women, working class women—all joined the struggle. Among them Kamala played a brave and noble role. Jawaharlal was arrested again and again during this time, and these prison terms came between him and Kamala.

Motilal died in 1931, leaving him as the head of the Nehru household.

Kamala was often ill. Finally she was sent to Europe for treatment. She entered a sanatorium at Badenweiler in the Black Forest in Germany. Jawaharlal was in prison at Almora in the mountains when news came in September 1935 that Kamala was in a critical condition. He was released and he went to Badenweiler to see her. She was still brave and smiling. Her condition took a turn for the better during December that year.

Jawaharlal went to England with Indira. Kamala's condition became bad again. She fought this crisis well also and was better and cheerful. She was tired of Badenweiler and wanted a change.

Jawaharlal had been elected president of the Congress for a second time and it was to meet in April. He did not want to leave Kamala; but she did not want him to resign from the

Jawaharlal, his wife and daughter, Indira

presidentship. In January 1936 when her condition improved, she was taken to a sanatorium in Switzerland. However, her recovery was slow. Jawaharlal consulted her and the doctor about his programme. He was to go back to India. But Kamala's condition was bad again and Jawaharlal had to postpone his return to India by a week or ten days. Early on the morning of February 28, Kamala died. A brave woman was gone. She was 37. In her brief lifespan Kamala Nehru made a lasting contribution to the Indian National movement.

5   Gandhi

Gandhi was a man of the centuries. Such men are born in this world only after long intervals. Some say he was the greatest Indian after the Buddha. He changed the face and mind of India. He made heroes of common men. He influenced many people of his time and the Nehru family was one of them. Motilal became a good friend of Gandhi, and Jawaharlal was his favourite disciple and his closest co-worker.

Mohandas Karamchand Gandhi was born in 1869 in Porbandar, a town in Kathiawad, which is now a part of Gujarat. His father and grandfather were dewans and his mother, Putlibai, was a devout and pious woman. Gandhi was much under her influence. He listened to her stories of great devotees, and was an honest and truthful boy. If he ever told a lie, he was ashamed of it and confessed. Whenever he did anything bad he did not conceal it. He was devoted to God and to truth; and he studied hard. At the age of thirteen he was married to Kasturba.

After his matriculation, Gandhi was sent to England to study for the Bar. He promised his mother he would not touch wine or meat. In London he learnt as much as he could. He led a simple life and kept an account of everything he spent. He dressed in English attire. He was a strict vegetarian and became a member of the Vegetarian Society. On his return to India in 1891, he practised in the courts for some time. He was then asked to take up a case in South Africa. He went there in 1893. He became deeply  interested in the struggle of the Indian people in South Africa for equal rights with the whites. He organized the Indians to fight for their rights. He was ill-treated and beaten by the whites, but he never gave up. In the long struggle he always followed truth and non-violence.

Gandhi thought much, read much, and wrote much. He edited weekly newspapers. He practised whatever he believed in even though he had to suffer a lot for this. Life to him was an experiment with truth. Truth was a part of the struggle which he led. Non-violence was another part of it. Gandhi waged his struggle against the whites in South Africa on a high level. The form of the struggle which Gandhi followed was known as Satyagraha. It means fasting to hold onto truth. Gandhi organized his fellow workers for Satyagraha. They were to follow truth and non-violence and live simply. Gandhi became known throughout the world.

Gandhi returned to India from South Africa in 1915 with a batch of volunteers. He took a vow of silence for one year. Then he began to speak on social, economic, and political problems. He spoke for greater use of Hindi and swadeshi, urging the people to use goods made in their own country; he spoke against untouchability and other evils; he preached the right to rebel. When war broke out he offered his cooperation to the British for some time. But the British did not concede self-government to India. Indian leaders demanded freedom. The British Government introduced laws for repression. When Indians protested, there was firing. The entire nation felt humiliated and angry.

Gandhi was a moderate at first, but in course of time he wanted a strong programme. He did not merely ask for political freedom. He wanted the people to be Indians in every sense, to boycott foreign cloth and foreign goods, to boycott schools and colleges and courts established by the British. This was called non-violent non-cooperation, meaning non-cooperation with the British regime.

From 1920 onwards, Gandhi became the greatest leader of the freedom movement. He was called Mahatma, or the Great Soul, because of his pure life. He insisted on the right ends and the right means. There were

Mahatma Gandhi and his wife, Kasturba, 1915

many leaders at that time but he soon led everyone. Thousands underwent a change. They wore khadi—hand-spun, hand-woven cloth; they gave up riches, and led simple lives. Gandhi had given up English clothes in South Africa. He wore only a turban and a dhoti when he returned to India. Now he started wearing only a loin cloth.

Motilal came under Gandhi's influence. From the princely life he had led, he changed to plain and simple living. He came close to Gandhi. Jawaharlal came even closer. Gandhi liked him the most amongst his associates. Jawaharlal was young, daring, chivalrous and truthful. Gandhi called him the jewel of India, and a man without reproach. Jawaharlal often differed from Gandhi. At first he could not understand Gandhi's ways. He could not understand non-violence; nor could he understand Gandhi's method of starting a struggle and calling it off if something went wrong. He often quarrelled with Gandhi. But, with the passing years, he began to understand Gandhi.

Gandhi was the spirit of India. Behind his simple ways was great strength. He was like a king, though he was meek. He was the leader of millions of Indians. He did not seem modern but he was a revolutionary. Among the leaders he alone had a plan of action. He showed the way. So, whatever his doubts, Jawaharlal followed him. They understood each other, loved each other, and worked together throughout Gandhi's life. And when Gandhi died, Jawaharlal felt that his Master was gone. He was on his own. But he never forgot Gandhi and what he and India owed to him. Even today whenever people think of Gandhi, they think of Jawaharlal. And whenever people think of Jawaharlal, they think of Gandhi. The two are indeed inseparable.

6   Freedom Struggle

The First World War ended in November 1918. The Indian people wanted freedom from the British rule and were in a mood of revolt. They asked the British to fulfil their promises. The British made new laws. Under these laws, people could be sent to prison without trial. Gandhi started Satyagraha. Congressmen disobeyed the law and got themselves arrested. This was their peaceful protest.

There was unrest throughout the country. One day, in 1919, people closed down all business for the day. There were police and military shootings at some places. In Amritsar, a crowd of people were listening to political leaders in a public garden called Jallianwala Bagh. The garden was surrounded by a wall. General Dyer opened fire on the crowd without warning. The assembled crowd could not escape because of the wall. Many people were killed. The Jallianwala Bagh massacre, as it came to be known as, is still remembered all over the country.

The Congress held an inquiry into the Jallianwala Bagh massacre. Jawaharlal went there with Gandhi and other leaders. They heard stories of horror. People had been flogged and made to crawl on their bellies even though they were innocent. The Congress' report on the massacre was written mainly by Gandhi. The British also held an inquiry. General Dyer was later punished. But he is still known as the man who killed many Indians without a cause.

Jawaharlal was in close touch with Gandhi those days. In 1919 there was a Congress session at Amritsar. There Gandhi was heard as a leader for the first time. He put forward his programme of non-violent non-cooperation. Gandhi thought that Indians themselves were responsible for not being free because they cooperated with the British. If they were to be free, they must not cooperate. They must at the same time be peaceful, for violence would lead to violence and would be bad. This was the idea behind non-violent non-cooperation. It was to begin on August 1, 1920. Unfortunately, Bal Gangadhar Tilak died on that day. Gandhi and Jawaharlal joined the vast funeral procession.

Many days later, Jawaharlal clashed with the authorities. His mother and his wife were not well and he took them to Mussoorie. An Afghan delegation had come to India for peace talks with the government. The Afghans too were fighting the British. The government did not want Jawaharlal to meet the Afghan delegation, and so ordered him to leave the district within twenty-four hours. Reluctantly, Jawaharlal returned to Allahabad.

At this time Jawaharlal came to know the peasants of the United Provinces. About two thousand of them were camping on the banks of the Yamuna. They asked him to hear the story of their sufferings. He heard them and was deeply moved. There were many landlords all over the United Provinces. They paid a tax to the government, but they could do what they liked with the land. They could not cultivate it themselves. The peasants cultivated it for them. But the landlords oppressed the peasants and collected as much money as possible from them. If they did not pay, they were driven off the land. They never knew how long they would be able to stay, nor when they might have to go. The peasants led miserable lives. Jawaharlal wanted them to rise against the landlords and help themselves. He spoke often to them. Jawaharlal gradually lost his shyness and began to address big meetings. The peasants helped him to know the countryside and Jawaharlal helped them to know themselves. The peasants joined the national movement in large numbers.

7   Non-cooperation

Non-cooperation became a great movement. It changed the lives of the people. They non-cooperated with everything that was British. They went to prison in large numbers. Many gave up foreign cloth and boycotted the schools and colleges that had been established by the British. National schools and colleges were established. Indian languages were encouraged. The Prince of Wales, the eldest son of the British king, came to India in 1921. Big receptions were arranged in his honour, but the people boycotted them. Jawaharlal was arrested while taking part in this boycott programme.

The non-cooperation movement went on and thousands of people were arrested. It seemed the movement was a great success. Then something bad happened. At Chauri Chaura, a village in Gorakhpur, Uttar Pradesh, a crowd of peasants set fire to a police station and burnt to death half a dozen policemen. Gandhi was very upset over this violence and withdrew the non-cooperation movement.

A family of freedom fighters: Jawaharlal, Kamala and Indira

In prison, Jawaharlal was unhappy over Gandhi's decision. What sort of leader was he? People had done a wrong thing at Chauri Chaura, and they had to be criticized. But why was the movement withdrawn? Jawaharlal felt it was difficult to understand Gandhi's strange ways. Motilal and other leaders also thought like Jawaharlal.

Jawaharlal was released from prison and he went to see Gandhi in Ahmedabad. He wanted to discuss with Gandhi what was to be done next. But before Jawaharlal reached Ahmedabad, Gandhi was arrested. Jawaharlal was present when Gandhi was tried and sentenced. Gandhi answered the charges made against him, and in answering them he made a statement which moved everyone. Even the British judge was moved.

Jawaharlal returned to Allahabad. He was arrested this time for picketing shops selling foreign cloth. He was sentenced to eighteen months' imprisonment. No one knew then when he would be set free or how long he would be allowed to remain free. But there was a lull in the non-cooperation movement, and many leaders were released. Jawaharlal kept himself busy. He became General Secretary of the Congress and held that post from time to time. He was hardworking and liked to take up challenges.

The British had introduced fresh reforms. There were new councils with ministers. The Congressmen did not want to be ministers and so Jawaharlal refused to be one. But some Congressmen thought they should be in the councils and fight for freedom from within. These Congressmen called themselves Swarajist for they wanted Swaraj or self-rule. The other Congressmen who did not want to fight elections or go into the councils thinking it would be a waste of time, were called

No-changers, or those who would not change. They wanted to follow Gandhi. Jawaharlal was one of them. He was for direct action, not for making speeches in the councils.

The Congressmen were thus divided and the members sometimes even criticized each other. But one thing was clear. They all respected Gandhi. He did not mind if they did not follow him. He knew they would come back to him. He did not like the programme of going into the councils. But he blessed the Swarajists also. The Swarajists gradually found that they could do nothing in the councils. They made speeches and they argued, but the British did not respond to the demand for Swaraj. They offered reforms, but they would not agree to give freedom.

8   Europe

There was confusion in the country. Nobody knew what would happen next. Gandhi was thinking of some plan of action, but he did not make up his mind. For Jawaharlal too there was no defined path. Kamala was ill and hospitalized in Lucknow. Now she needed treatment in Switzerland. In March 1926 Jawaharlal, Kamala and Indira left for Europe.

Jawaharlal was happy to get away from India. He wanted to see things from a distance. He enjoyed his visit to Europe. He enjoyed it in every way, going to old places, meeting old friends, and taking part in sports. He liked to keep himself in good health, wherever he was. This habit remained with him throughout his lifetime.

There were several Indians who had left India and were living in Europe—people from all walks of life. Jawaharlal enjoyed meeting these men who had fought for their country their own way. He also met another set of people, people like Romain Rolland, the French writer, and Ernst Toller, the German dramatist.

In February 1927 the Congress of Oppressed

Nationalities met in Brussels. The Indian National Congress nominated Jawaharlal as a delegate to the Brussels meeting. Many leaders of who became famous later were there. Jawaharlal met the widow of Sun Yat Sen, the great leader of China, who had brought freedom and a modern outlook to that country. Madame Sun Yat Sen was to become a leader of the regime set up by the Communists in China. Jawaharlal also met Dr. Ho Chi-Minh, the leader of the Vietnamese people who were struggling against French rule. Dr. Ho was to become the President of North Vietnam. Jawaharlal also met other leaders. They differed in their views on the means but they all wanted freedom from colonial rule.

At Brussels, Jawaharlal understood India's freedom struggle against the background of the freedom struggle

As a delegate to the Congress of Oppressed Nationalities in Brussels, 1927

of others who were also under foreign rule. This experience helped him to understand that the struggle was the same all over the world.

Jawaharlal also went to the Soviet Union. There he found a new civilization, a new way of life. He had studied the Russian Revolution which had taken place in 1917, but now he saw for himself what changes it had brought to the Russian people. The visit made a big impression on him. He worked for friendship between India and the Soviet Union. He wanted India to learn from the Soviet Union's experience.

9   Independence Pledge

Jawaharlal returned from Europe full of new ideas. At the Madras Congress, in December 1927, he moved a resolution saying Independence was India's goal. Till then, Congress leaders had been prepared to think of India as a dominion within the British Empire. A dominion was free except for some link with the British Crown. Dominion status meant a substance of Independence. The Congress now said that India should be completely independent. Gandhi thought Jawaharlal was rash and criticized him.

At this time, the British Government decided to find out if India was fit for self-rule or Swaraj. It appointed a commission of inquiry called the Simon Commission. Simon, a famous lawyer, was its chairman. There were no Indians on the commission. The Congress and other nationalist parties in India decided to boycott it. When the commission came to India, a large number of people, old and young, greeted them with shouts of: "Simon, Go Back!" The Congress leaders led the boycott and Jawaharlal was one of them.

During a demonstration against the Simon Commission, Jawaharlal was attacked by mounted police in Lucknow. He wanted to hit back. It was difficult to remain non-violent when beaten with lathis. But Gandhi wanted the people to be non-violent. So Jawaharlal faced the blows bravely though he was badly hurt. There was a stir throughout the country.

The British threw a challenge to the Indian people. The Indian people seemed divided and the British asked them to prepare an agreed scheme for self-rule. A conference of all parties was held under Motilal's chairmanship. It prepared a scheme. But the British did not accept it. They wanted the Simon Commission to prepare a scheme. The commission prepared one, but the Indian people did not want it.

The Congress met at Calcutta in December 1928. Motilal was the president. There were differences between the older and the younger people. The older people were led by Gandhi and Motilal. The younger people were led by Jawaharlal and Subhas Bose. Jawaharlal and Subhas wanted immediate Independence. The older leaders did not want to be in a hurry. They thought India was not in a position to enforce a demand for Independence. There was a compromise. The British were to be given one year's notice. If they did not agree to Independence within one year, the Congress

Gandhi with Sardar Patel

would declare Independence as its goal.

The one year passed. There was no response from the British. The Viceroy, Lord Irwin, held talks with the leaders, but he did not agree even to dominion status. The Congress was to meet at Lahore. Jawaharlal was chosen to preside over the meeting. Other names were proposed, but Gandhi was keen on Jawaharlal becoming president. This was what Gandhi said of him at this time, "In bravery, he is not to be surpassed. Who can excel him in the love of the country? ...He is undoubtedly an extremist, thinking far ahead of his surrounding. But he is humble enough and practical enough not to force the pace to the breaking point. He is pure as the crystal, he is truthful beyond suspicion... The nation is safe in his hands."

Jawaharlal was only forty when he presided at Lahore. He rode on a white horse to the Congress platform. He made a spirited speech:

"I am a socialist and a republican," he said. He did not care for kings and for captains of industry. He wanted Swaraj for the poor, not for the rich. He urged the people to dare and to act. At midnight on December 31, 1929, the Congress declared their call for Independence and the Congressmen took the Independence Pledge. It was indeed a historic day.

President, Lahore Congress, 1929

10   Salt Satyagraha

The Congress took the Independence Pledge, but there was no response from the British. A plan of action was necessary and Gandhi had a plan. He put forward proposals for reform. One of them was that there should be no tax on salt. If the proposals were not accepted, there would be Satyagraha. The Viceroy rejected the proposals. Gandhi prepared the country for Satyagraha.

It was a strange Satyagraha. Gandhi felt that salt was the poor man's food and there should he no tax on it. It should be free. So he asked the people to make salt illegally. The salt law was to be broken. It would not bring Swaraj, but Gandhi thought of it as an effective form of protest and decided that he himself would lead it.

On March 12, 1930, Gandhi marched with a band of volunteers from his ashram at Sabarmati towards Dandi. He stopped at the wayside villages and spoke to the people. "Today the pilgrim marches onward on his long trek..." said Jawaharlal.

The Salt Satyagraha began. Large numbers of people, including many women, started making salt. They were

The Dandi March: Gandhi and his followers on their way to the seashore

arrested or beaten with lathis. But they continued to
break the law. Jawaharlal was arrested and sentenced
at Allahabad. Gandhi was arrested on reaching Dandi.
Motilal was arrested and put in the same prison as
Jawaharlal at Naini. Other leaders were also arrested.
New leaders sprang up everywhere, and the Satyagraha
went on.

The British Government found that the Satyagraha
was a success. So they opened talks with the Congress
leaders. The Viceroy released Motilal and Jawaharlal.
They went to Poona and met Gandhi. Their joint
demands were rejected by the Viceroy. The Nehrus
returned to Naini prison. Motilal fell ill and was released.
He went to Mussoorie. Jawaharlal was also released so
that he could be with his father. When he returned to

Allahabad, Jawaharlal was arrested. Motilal fell ill again. Gandhi and Jawaharlal rushed to his bedside. As Motilal was being taken to Lucknow from Mussoorie, he died on February 6, 1931. Gandhi felt he had lost his closest friend. Jawaharlal was grief-stricken. He was now on his own.

Motilal had lived a full life and given much to the nation. He had given up a princely life for a life of suffering. He had been a great patriot and a great leader, a king among men. He even gave his palatial house, Anand Bhawan, to the nation re-naming it Swaraj Bhawan. Later he built a new house for his family and which was called Anand Bhawan. It is now a place of pilgrimage.

There were talks in London between the British Government and moderate Indian leaders who went to London. These talks were called the Round Table Conferences. At the first conference, Congress leaders were not present. They were still in prison and they refused to take part in it. Gandhi attended the second conference after an agreement with the Viceroy. This was called the Gandhi-Irwin Agreement. Some called it a truce, for reasons there might be a struggle again between the British and the Congress. The Viceroy agreed to Gandhi's conditions. The Congress met at Karachi and decided to send Gandhi to London as its only representative. He went there in his loin cloth, charmed everyone, and made stirring speeches. But the British were in no mood to grant Swaraj. The second Round Table Conference was a failure. Gandhi was disappointed.

In India, the Gandhi-Irwin Agreement was broken. Jawaharlal was blamed for it by the British and by the moderates. But the officials did not want the agreement to succeed. The peasants were in revolt in the United

The Second Round Table Conference in London in 1931.
In the picture can be seen Gandhi, Pandit Madan Mohan Malaviya,
Śrinivasa Shastri and Tej Bahadur Sapru

Provinces. Jawaharlal led them. The government would not allow any movement. Jawaharlal was arrested. Gandhi heard about it when he was returning from London. He himself was arrested soon after landing on Indian soil.

The third Round Table Conference met in London without the Congress.

11   Life in Prison

Jawaharlal loved action and often his views clashed with the government. For this he was arrested many times and spent many years of his life in prison. He was in different prisons at Naini, Bareilly, Dehra Dun, Almora, Alipore in Calcutta, and Ahmadnagar. It was hard to be cut off from life, to be away from the family, and to be lonely. Prison conditions were always bad. The prison officials were usually courteous and allowed him to receive journals and books. But prison was prison and the atmosphere was sometimes unbearable.

Jawaharlal did not become bitter because of his life in prison. He bore no grudge. He tried to make the best use of his time in prison. He followed a strict discipline. He regularly exercised to keep himself physically fit. He also did a lot of tough mental work so that his mind was always fresh. Days and weeks and months passed. A few interviews were allowed, and they were precious. There were fortnightly letters from home or from friends in other prisons, and they were precious too. He had companions sometimes, but most of the time he was alone. He did gardening and loved it. He would also spin a little every day. He watched birds and animals. He read much and wrote much. Novels made him mentally slack and he read few of them. He liked travel books and books containing pictures, especially of mountains and glaciers and deserts.

Jawaharlal was a great writer. He was considered one of the finest writers of English. He did his best writing in prison. He had time and his mind had some rest there. From 1931 to 1933, he wrote letters from time to time to his little daughter, Indira. These letters conveyed history, from the beginning till modem times. Jawaharlal wrote mainly from memory but he seemed to remember everything. He wrote of the old civilizations, the revolutions which had changed the course of history, and the social and economic problems of the world. The letters were later published in the form of a book called *Glimpses of World History.* It is one of the finest histories of the world in one book.

Jawaharlal also wrote his autobiography in prison. The book *Jawaharlal Nehru: an autobiography* was written between June 1934 and February 1935 and was published in 1936 in England. It became famous immediately. It was sold and read widely. Its frankness and charm impressed the world. Certain portions of it read like poetry. Jawaharlal wrote the book at a difficult period in his life, when his mind was troubled and he had many doubts. He criticized Gandhi and others freely. But he wrote honestly and with modesty and he put himself many questions. It was both an account of himself and a history of the times. It is one of the best autobiographies.

Jawaharlal was imprisoned in Ahmadnagar Fort in 1942 and had to stay there for nearly three years. There he wrote another book: *The Discovery of India.* This, too, became very famous. The book deals with India's past history, both with its problems past and present, and gives a glimpse of the future. It is living history. The past comes back to life in Jawaharlal's pages. He had widely travelled the country and knew a lot about people from different parts.

In Naini Jail, 1930

He realized how diverse they were in their food and habits, yet how similar they were as citizen of one country. He discovered India and her people, and the book shows his great love for them. Jawaharlal's life in prison was not wasted. He made the best use of his time. He wrote three great books while he was in prison.

12   Lucknow
                    and Faizpur

There was a lull in the freedom struggle. There was severe repression and the people were angry but helpless. The Viceroy, Lord Willingdon, used harsh measures. After Gandhi's return from London, he and Jawaharlal were frequently in and out of prison.

On August 17, 1932, the British Government announced their decision to treat the untouchables as a separate community and grant them separate electorates. The decision was called the Communal Award. Gandhi, in prison, protested and went on a fast. Thereafter he was released. After much negotiation it was agreed that the Communal Award would be withdrawn. The untouchables would remain a part of the Hindu community. Gandhi called them Harijans, the people of 'Hari', that is, God. Everyone now knows them as Harijans. Gandhi devoted himself to their welfare. If India was to be free, they were to be free, he said.

Jawaharlal was released in August 1933 when his

mother was seriously ill. When her health improved, he used his freedom to meet Gandhi and other leaders and to attend to domestic affairs. It was known he might be arrested again soon. So he decided to go to Calcutta for consultations about Kamala's health.

On January 15, 1934, there was a big earthquake in Bihar. Large parts of the province were in ruins. Many people suffered. From Calcutta Jawaharlal went to Bihar to see to the relief operations. He condemned the government for their incompetence and inefficiency in organizing relief. When he returned to Allahabad, he was arrested. The warrant of arrest had been sent from Calcutta where he had made strong speeches. He was taken to Calcutta and kept in the Presidency Prison and tried there where he was sentenced to two years imprisonment. He was later transferred to Alipore Central Prison.

At first he did not like the atmosphere of the prison. But gradually he got accustomed to the conditions in Alipore and to the climate of Calcutta.

In May he was transferred to the prison at Dehra Dun with its nearby mountains. In the new atmosphere he read much. He watched nature in action, and he thought of the world and its problems. There in June 1934 he started writing his autobiography.

Towards the end of July, Kamala's condition worsened and within a few days she was critical. On August 11, Jawaharlal was asked to leave Dehra Dun and was sent under police escort to Allahabad. This freedom did not last long.

On August 25 he was arrested again and sent to Naini Prison. Some weeks later he was transferred to the district prison at Almora so that he could be nearer to Kamala who was at Bhowali for treatment. In November he was forty-five and he thought he had still many years to live. On February 11, 1935, he completed writing his autobiography.

In September 1935 he was suddenly discharged from Almora Prison to enable him to join Kamala who had been taken to Germany in May the same year. Jawaharlal watched the rise of Hitler to absolute power in Germany. In Italy Mussolini had long been a dictator. Both Hitler and Mussolini threatened to disturb the peace. After Kamala's death in February 1936 Jawaharlal returned to India to preside over the Congress session at Lucknow.

On his way back from Europe Jawaharlal passed through Rome. Mussolini, the Italian dictator, wanted to see him but he refused to go.

At Lucknow Jawaharlal spoke not only of the freedom struggle in India but of the larger struggle for freedom in the world. He had seen the forces of aggression rise in Europe. Britain and other countries were imperialist powers. All over the world they held down many peoples, such as the Indians.

Italy had an empire and, under Mussolini, was threatening to grab more territory. Germany, under Hitler, was threatening the peace of other countries. In the East Japan was taking over large parts of China. Jawaharlal presented this picture of the world to the Congress delegates at Lucknow. They began to understand for the first time that there could be no peace in the world if there was no peace in any part of it.

They learnt that India's freedom struggle was a part of the freedom struggle of peoples all over the world. Jawaharlal taught the Congress and India to develop a world outlook.

Jawaharlal also preached socialism. Socialism meant

the people's control of public wealth and equal opportunities for all. There were princes and zamindars on one side and the backward and downtrodden people on the other. There were the rich people on one side and the poor on the other. Jawaharlal said that India must establish social and economic equality. This could not be done in a short time. But the ideal must be kept in mind. Many Congressmen did not like Jawaharlal's ideas, but he went on presenting them boldly.

Jawaharlal was also fighting communalism. People were Hindus or Muslims, Sikhs or Christians. They thought as Hindus or as Muslims, as Sikhs or as Christians. This promoted separatism and Jawaharlal felt that it would be harmful for the growth of the nation. He condemned communal organizations. He wanted the people to be Indians above all, above community, above caste. He did not pretend to be a religious person, but he did not mind others following whatever religion they liked. But religion had to be put in its proper place. It must be kept separate from politics and must not be allowed to divide people. This is called secularism. It is also the scientific spirit. Jawaharlal asked the people to cast away old ideas and old habits. He wanted them to know they were living in modem times, in the age of science, and must possess modern minds.

As Congress president, Jawaharlal continued to spread his ideas. The peasants and labourers liked him. The youth adored him; he was their idol. Among Congress leaders, he was the closest to Gandhi. He was very popular and he was asked to be Congress president for one more year. So he presided over the Congress session at Faizpur also. His friend, Subhas Bose, presided over the Congress session in 1938 at Haripura in Gujarat. But there were differences between

Subhas Bose

Subhas Bose and other Congress leaders. He was elected again the following year but he resigned. Subhas Bose later left the country to fight for India's freedom from abroad.

13   Europe Again

The sound of war drums was heard in Europe. Events were moving fast. Hitler gained control over Austria and threatened to take over part of Czechoslovakia. Benito Mussolini of Italy invaded Albania in 1939. In Spain a civil war was raging fiercely. The people there had overthrown the king and established a republic. But a General named Francisco Franco y Bahamonde landed with troops to overthrow the republic. Franco used foreign troops and the republicans were fighting a losing battle. Mussolini helped Franco.

Like many other people, Jawaharlal was stirred by the struggle of the Spanish republic. People from various countries went to Spain and fought by the side of the republicans. Jawaharlal had a great desire to see the struggle and to express his sympathy. He went to Spain and moved about the trenches with republican soldiers.

Jawaharlal then went to Vienna, Prague, Budapest, and other places. He saw Fascist and Nazi forces threatening peace everywhere. The Fascists were Mussolini's party; they did not allow any other party to

In Spain during the Civil War

function. The Nazis were national socialists who followed Hitler. They talked of socialism, but they supported the rich against the workers. Both Mussolini and Hitler were dictators and could do what they liked. They not only had the armed forces of their countries under their control but private armies of their own as well. They suppressed all opposition by violence and terror. They paid more attention to guns than to bread for the people. They threatened peace. Hitler wanted to take over as many countries as possible. He believed that the Germans were a superior race and had a right to rule over others.

Jawaharlal hated Fascism and Nazism. But he also disliked the policy of Britain and France. They did nothing to stop Hitler from threatening small countries like Czechoslovakia and Poland. They allowed Mussolini to help Franco in Spain against the rightful government. In September 1938 they entered into an agreement with

Hitler at Munich. Under this agreement they allowed Hitler to take over part of Czechoslovakia. They said they were doing it for the sake of peace. But people all over the world denounced it as a cowardly surrender. Britain and France were afraid of having to fight Hitler, and they gave in. Jawaharlal denounced the Munich Pact bitterly. His sympathy was with Czechoslovakia. The Prime Minister of Britain at that time was Neville Chamberlain, and Jawaharlal felt contempt for him. Jawaharlal's actions in those days are still remembered by the brave people of Czechoslovakia and by other victims of Fascism and Nazism.

Jawaharlal returned to India with his mind full of the events in Europe. He knew there would be war. He knew that India would be drawn into it. He wanted the people to think of the whole world and what part they should play in it.

Hitler did not rest with Munich. He violated that agreement and took over the whole of Czechoslovakia. He was threatening Poland. Britain and France gave a guarantee that they would help Poland if Hitler attacked her.

Jawaharlal went on a visit to China in 1939 to see how the war was going on there. He had sent a medical mission to China to express India's sympathy with her. He now himself went to express the sympathy of the Indian people with the Chinese. While he was in China, Hitler attacked Poland, and there was war in Europe.

14 World War

War broke out in Europe in September 1939 and spread to the whole world. It was called the Second World War. Jawaharlal cut short his visit to China and returned. He saw clearly what the war meant. The British were fighting Hitler but they were really fighting in defence of their empire. It was not India's war. The British had drawn the Indian people into it without their consent. At the same time, Hitler represented evil, and Jawaharlal did not want Hitler to win. It was a difficult situation, but Jawaharlal's mind was clear.

Jawaharlal wanted India also to fight against Hitler. But it was only a free India that could do so. If India fought against Hitler without being free, she would be fighting in defence of imperialism. So Jawaharlal wanted India to be declared free. The Viceroy, Lord Linlithgow, rejected the offer of cooperation on those terms. India was asked to wait for freedom till the end of the war.

The Congress had formed ministries in 1937 in some provinces. They now resigned. Gandhi asked people not to cooperate with the British in the war effort. To make the protest effective, he started a No-war Satyagraha in July 1940. Vinoba Bhave was selected as the first Satyagrahi. He was a worker in Gandhi's ashram and now came to be widely known for the first time. Jawaharlal was to be the second Satyagrahi. He represented the political side.

Vinoba and others were arrested. Before Jawaharlal could offer Satyagraha, he was arrested for some speeches he had made in Gorakhpur. He was tried at that place and sentenced to four years' imprisonment. The sentence was so severe that it shocked the country and was condemned even in England. Gandhi himself was arrested in October 1940. The Satyagraha went on. Thousands of Congress workers were in prison. The war effort went on too, but it was clear that the people had nothing to do with the war.

The war was yet distant from India, though Hitler conquered France and other countries and attacked the Soviet Union. But in December 1941 Japan entered the war, destroyed a large part of the American fleet at Pearl Harbour in a surprise attack, and swiftly conquered many countries in the Far East. America entered the war immediately after Pearl Harbour and the war now spread to the whole world. When Japan conquered Malaya and Burma, the war was brought to India's borders. The British Government now felt they could not defend India without the cooperation of the Indian people. They released the Congress leaders.

The British sent proposals to India through a senior minister, Sir Stafford Cripps. They were called the Cripps Proposals. They offered some power to the Indian people during the period of the war and freedom after the war. But the Indian people were not yet trusted. They were not offered the power to defend themselves. Gandhi rejected the British proposals outright. Jawaharlal was anxious that India should fight against Hitler, Mussolini, and Japan, and was prepared to negotiate. But he wanted real power immediately so that the Indian people could defend themselves and defend the forces of freedom. But Cripps and the British Government did not agree. Even if Indians had other powers, they would not have control of defence.

There were differences among the Congress leaders. Gandhi stuck to non-violence, even for defence. Jawaharlal and most other Congress leaders wanted to use force for defence. Japanese forces might invade India at any moment. Gandhi wanted only non-violence to be used. Jawaharlal wanted India to be defended with force. But the leaders did not quarrel. They were all agreed that India must be free and that she must be given power immediately.

Some people thought there was a split between Gandhi and Jawaharlal. Both of them denied it.

Jawaharlal said there could be no break with Gandhi, for he represented the mind and heart of the Indian people as no one else could. Gandhi said, "Jawaharlal will be my successor. He says that he does not understand my language and that he speaks a language foreign to me. This may or may not be true. But language is no bar to a union of hearts. And I know this, that when I am gone he will speak my language."

Gandhi and Sir Stafford Cripps

15   Quit India

The situation was desperate. The British armies were in retreat everywhere. The Japanese could attack India any moment. But the British would not agree to give freedom. They said they would transfer power only after the war, if the Indian people agreed among themselves. But they proposed a scheme which could only keep the Indian people divided.

Some Muslims had a separate organization. It was called the Muslim League. It demanded a separate homeland for Muslims. That would mean partition of the country. Hinduism and Islam were different religions, but Hindus and Muslims were one people. They spoke the same language, had the same habits, and had the same needs and desires. But the Muslim League and its leader, Jinnah, said that the Muslims were a separate nation and must have a separate State. This was called the two-nation theory. The Congress did not accept it. To Gandhi and Jawaharlal there could be no separation between Hindus and Muslims. Two religions did not mean two nations and there was no need for two States.

Nehru and Mohammad Ali Jinnah

The British encouraged the Muslim League. It grew in strength.

Gandhi wanted to press the British for freedom. So he gave the slogan 'Quit India'. The British must quit India, whatever happened. The Indian people could unite only if the British left. They would settle their problems among themselves. Freedom alone would unite them. Gandhi was in a mood for action. He was writing strong articles in strong language. Jawaharlal liked the prospect of action.

On August 8, 1942, the Congress met in Bombay and passed the 'Quit India' resolution. Gandhi and

Jawaharlal made powerful speeches. Gandhi wanted freedom so that the Indian people could unite and solve their problems. Jawaharlal wanted freedom so that the Indian people could fight in defence of world freedom.

The day after the Congress passed the resolution, the British Government arrested Gandhi and all the other leaders. Gandhi was put in the Aga Khan's Palace near Poona. Jawaharlal, Sardar Patel, Maulana Azad and Rajendra Prasad were sent to Ahmadnagar Fort. There were uprisings all over the country and there was severe repression. The people were in revolt. They had no leaders and no plan of action. Thousands were sent to prison, thousands of rupees were collected as fines. Many were shot, some were hanged. It was the biggest revolt in the country after 1857.

In February 1943 Gandhi began a fast. The government carried on a propaganda saying that he had been responsible for the disturbances in the country. He repudiated this propaganda. His health was not good and he nearly died. But he lived through it. In prison, Kasturba and his beloved disciple, Mahadev Desai, died. Their deaths meant a great loss to Gandhi.

The British and their allies were now winning battles. Hitler was exhausted by the war against the Soviet Union, and the Americans were turning the Japanese back. Gandhi was released in May 1944. He held talks with Jinnah, seeking an agreement between the Congress and the Muslim League. The talks failed.

In 1945 the war ended. In July the Labour Party came to power in Britain. They wanted to make another attempt to settle India's demand for freedom. There were signs that Britain would not be able to hold India after the war. There had been a great famine in Bengal and lakhs of people had died. Subhas Bose had

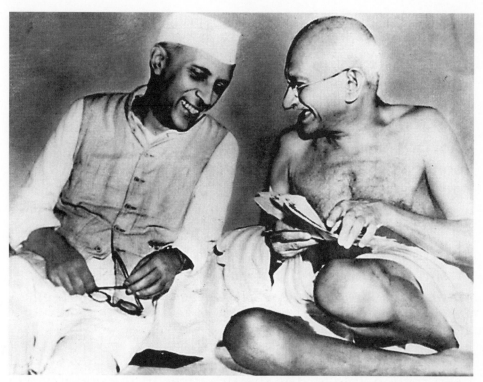

A talk with Gandhi

organized an army from Indian prisoners of war taken by the Japanese, and they had fought bravely. That army was defeated but the Indian people were full of admiration for it. The British thought there might be unrest in the Indian army. There was a mutiny by Indian ratings in the Navy and the warning was clear—the British would not be able to hold India for long.

16   Partition

The war in Europe came to an end. In the summer of 1945 the new Viceroy, Lord Wavell, released Jawaharlal and other leaders. He held talks in Simla (now Shimla) with representatives of leading parties for a political settlement. Gandhi was present. But nothing came out of the talks. Jinnah insisted that the Muslim League alone represented the Muslims. The Congress said that it also represented the Muslims.

The war in the Far East was going on. The Americans had made the atom bomb, and they dropped one first on Hiroshima and then another on Nagasaki in Japan. The two bombs caused terrible destruction. The Japanese surrendered and the war in the Far East also ended. But there was great shock throughout the world that an atom bomb had been used.

Jawaharlal was full of pride at the resistance shown by the Indian people to the British might after the leaders had been arrested. He felt that freedom was near and that the British could not further delay it. The Soviet Union was now a leading power. America was another.

They both stood against imperialism and they did not want Britain to rule India any longer. But the difficulty was to make the Muslim League agree to the transfer of power to Indian hands. The Muslim League insisted on partition of the country and every British plan seemed to support it.

Partition made no sense to Jawaharlal. How could there be partition when Hindus and Muslims lived in the same villages and religion made no difference? And how many partitions were there to be? India was to consist of free units. If any part of the country did not want to join the Indian Union, it could not be compelled to do so. Every part of the country had to be a willing unit. Yet partition had to be avoided; there should never be partition on the basis of religion.

In February 1946 the British Government sent a cabinet mission to India. It consisted of three senior cabinet ministers, Lord Pethick-Lawrence, A. V. Alexander, and Sir Stafford Cripps, Jawaharlal's old friend. They held talks with Indian leaders and made two sets of proposals—long-term and short-term.

Under the long-term proposals, there was to be a Constitution-making body, or a Constituent Assembly.

British Cabinet Mission with Lord Wavell, Viceroy, in New Delhi

Jawaharlal had demanded this long ago on the basis of what was called self-determination. Every people must be free to determine their future. The Indian people were to be free to frame their Constitution. But, under the long-term proposals, some parts of the country were to be free not to join the Indian Union; they could remain separate. This meant partition. The Congress accepted the long-term proposals with the hope that partition could be avoided.

The short-term proposals were for an interim national government to work till the Constitution was framed. It was called an interim government because it was to be provisional and was not to be based on the strength of parties. The government was to consist of the representatives of the Congress and the Muslim League, and others.

The Muslim League did not accept the short-term proposals because Jawaharlal had said that the Congress would go into the Constituent Assembly to shape Indian freedom as it liked. The Muslim League said the Congress had rejected the long-term proposals and so had no right to form an interim national government

Jawaharlal was president of the Congress at this time, and the Congress accepted the short-term proposals. So Lord Wavell appointed Jawaharlal as vice-president of the Viceroy's Executive Council. The vice-president and the other members were to work as a cabinet. The vice-president presided over it and was, in a sense, Prime Minister. Jawaharlal invited not only leading Congressmen but others, especially representatives of minority communities, to join the government. Jawaharlal showed great zeal and enthusiasm in his work. He worked like a Prime Minister. Sardar Patel,

Rajendra Prasad, and Maulana Azad were members of the government.

After some months the Viceroy persuaded the Muslim League to join the government. Some members were dropped from the Executive Council and Muslim League members joined it. But they obstructed business and did not cooperate with Jawaharlal. They wanted to force partition. The Constituent Assembly met in November. Jawaharlal made fine speeches there and laid down broad social and economic objectives. He gave shape and content to freedom. The Constituent Assembly went on with its work, though the Muslim League did not enter it.

The British Government thought that things could not continue as they were. They decided to transfer power to the Indian people before June 1948, whatever happened. Lord Mountbatten, a distinguished admiral, was appointed the new Viceroy. He held discussions with the Indian leaders, and then went to London and prepared, in consultation with the British Government, a fresh plan of action. It was called the June 3 Plan.

Under the plan, the country was to be partitioned. India and Pakistan were to be two separate countries from August 15, 1947. The date of freedom was advanced. Partition was accepted by both the Congress and the Muslim League. But the Muslim League did not get what it had wanted. The largely Hindu parts of Bengal and Punjab came to India, and so did Assam. It was a smaller Pakistan that Jinnah had wanted.

Gandhi was much against this partition. So was Jawaharlal. But Jawaharlal and other Congress leaders felt that freedom could not be postponed further. The people must be free immediately to shape their future as they liked. Also, unwilling units could not be forced

Members of the Interim National Government, 1946

into the Indian Union. The Congress could not fight both
Britain and the Muslim League forever. Jawaharlal felt
that freedom, even on the basis of partition, was better
than a permanent division within the country, even if it
was free. It was better to have a Pakistan outside than
inside. To Jawaharlal, it was succession, a separation,
not partition. Gandhi did not want to stand in the way.

Jawaharlal and other Congress leaders felt that
separation would be smooth and friendly. But the
Muslim League did not cooperate. There were many
communal riots in northern India. Muslims fled from
India, and Hindus fled from Pakistan. There was much
bloodshed and suffering and much bitterness between
the two countries.

17   Independence

On August 15, 1947, Jawaharlal was sworn in as the first Prime Minister of free India. He was fifty-eight, and he looked young and fit and cheerful. The pledge of freedom had been fulfilled. The people were free to build their future.

In a speech in the Constituent Assembly on August 14, Jawaharlal said, "Long years ago, we made a tryst with destiny. Now the time comes when we shall redeem our pledge. We have to build the noble mansion of free India where all our children may dwell." In a broadcast to the nation on August 15, he described himself as the first servant of the Indian people.

There was a long shadow cast across the new freedom. Bengal and Punjab were gravely disturbed with thousands of Hindus and Muslims killed or uprooted and driven out. There was Hindu-Muslim tension in other places in the north. Gandhi had toured villages in East Pakistan to comfort the people. Now he was busy in Bihar and Delhi. Jawaharlal rushed from place to place to prevent the killing of Muslims. He sometimes

Jawaharlal Nehru being sworn in as Prime Minister, 1947

rushed bravely into the streets of Delhi at grave risk to his life. It was a matter of faith for him. Gandhi preached peace daily at his prayer meetings. He went on a fast for peace between Hindus and Muslims. The leaders of the two communities promised that peace would be kept and he broke his fast.

One evening a bomb was thrown at his prayer meeting. Gandhi went on preaching his message. On January 30, 1948, he was shot dead by a young man named Nathuram Godse. The nation was shocked. Gandhi had given his life for communal unity.

Jawaharlal, in a message broadcast to the people, said, "The light has gone out of our lives and there is darkness everywhere... The light has gone out, I said, and yet I was wrong. For the light that shone in this country was no ordinary light. The light that has illumined this country for these many, many years will illumine this country for many more years, and a thousand years later, that light will be seen in this country and the world will see it."

The whole world paid homage to Gandhi. The nation was in mourning. Jawaharlal felt lonely without Gandhi.

There were big tasks ahead and Jawaharlal could not afford to relax or rest. The refugees had to be housed and fed. Partition had created difficult problems between India and Pakistan. Pakistan's leaders had wanted Pakistan but they were not reconciled to the results of partition. It left Pakistan a smaller country with smaller resources. This bred an inferiority complex among Pakistani leaders. India still had more than fifty million Muslims. It was still the biggest Muslim country in the world after Indonesia and Pakistan. These Muslims enjoyed equal rights with other citizens belonging to other religions. But with much communal tension, Jawaharlal had to assert that India belonged to men of all religions. This was the secular outlook. The country was above any particular religion.

The Indian people were free but they had to make a Constitution for themselves. Jawaharlal took a leading part in the shaping of the Constitution. The Constitution was that of a sovereign democratic republic. All people were to have equal rights. Freedom of thought and expression was ensured. There was to be social and economic justice. Jawaharlal moved in the Constituent

Assembly the resolution on objectives which gave shape to the Constitution. It took nearly two years to complete it.

On January 26, 1950, the Constitution came into effect. Rajendra Prasad became the first President of the republic. India was to have no monarch. But the British Commonwealth agreed to have a republic as a member, and India remained in the Commonwealth. The head of the Commonwealth is the British Sovereign. This was a

Signing the Constitution of the Indian Republic, 1950

concession made by India for the sake of the unity of the Commonwealth. It did not restrict India's freedom. Other Asian and African countries followed India, and the British Empire became a Commonwealth of free nations.

The British had left India free but divided. There were nearly six hundred princes in India with big or small territories, but each with ruling powers. They were all under the British power, but when the British were leaving India they said the princes were independent and could join India or Pakistan, as they wished.

Jawaharlal had worked among the subjects of the princes and these people had grown in strength; and the princes were not strong enough to make themselves independent. Almost all of them who were within Indian territory agreed to join the Indian Union, because they knew their people would not allow them to remain apart. Sardar Patel, as the first Home Minister and Deputy Prime Minister, did good work in making the princes agree. There was trouble only in Hyderabad and in Kashmir. Police action was taken against Hyderabad and then Hyderabad joined the Indian Union. Some people from Pakistan attacked Kashmir to force the ruler to join Pakistan. But the ruler joined the Indian Union and India had to send troops to defend Kashmir.

With Sardar Patel, Deputy Prime Minister

74

18 Kashmir and Pakistan

Jawaharlal's ancestors had come from Kashmir but he himself had nothing to do directly with that State. He visited it often and loved it for its beautiful valleys and snow-clad mountaintops. Kashmir had been made for peace, but there was conflict. The Maharaja of Jammu and Kashmir could not decide whether to join India or Pakistan. Every other ruler had made his decision. The rulers whose States were in Indian territory joined the Indian Union, and the rulers whose States were in Pakistan territory joined Pakistan. Kashmir was between India and Pakistan and its ruler could join either country. But he did not decide quickly.

India was prepared to wait, but the rulers of Pakistan would not. Towards the end of 1947 they organized raiders from the tribal people of the North-West Frontier and sent them across the border into Kashmir. These people looted villages and killed people and were advancing on Srinagar, the capital. The people were in

Enjoying a ride in Kashmir

a state of alarm. The Maharaja fled in panic. At this time he declared that his State was joining the Indian Union. India could not remain inactive. Jawaharlal and Sardar Patel decided that Kashmir must be defended against the raiders. Gandhi blessed their action and troops were sent.

India did not like the use of force, but she had to defend Kashmir by force. She declared that as soon as peace was established, there would be a reference to the people about the future of Kashmir.

Indian troops were flown into Srinagar at a short notice but they successfully repelled the Pakistani raiders. Pakistan said that the people who looted villages had acted on their own, but soon Pakistani troops were also in action. India was in a position to drive out the Pakistanis completely from Kashmir. But to do so she would have to attack the bases in Pakistan. This might lead to war between India and Pakistan, and India did not want a war. She had great faith in the United Nations, and early in 1948 she made a complaint to the Security Council, the most important organ of the United Nations.

India said that Pakistan should not send raiders or help them in any way and that the Kashmir question should be settled peacefully. The Security Council did not deal directly with India's complaint. Britain and America especially ignored India's charge of Pakistani aggression. They treated India and Pakistan as equal parties. The Security Council appointed a commission which was to bring about first a truce in Kashmir and then an agreement on how to find out the wishes of the people about Kashmir's future. The commission affirmed Pakistan's aggression and said that Pakistan had concealed the fact that she had sent troops. Under the commission's resolutions, Pakistan's forces were to be withdrawn from Kashmir. India would exercise control, and then the people would decide whether to join India or Pakistan. The means of finding out the people's wishes was loosely called a plebiscite.

India could have driven out the Pakistani troops by force. But for the sake of peace she had made a complaint to the Security Council. No justice was done to that complaint, and Jawaharlal was disappointed. He agreed to a truce, under protest. For him, peace was important, and he did not want war with Pakistan. A ceasefire line was established. In law, the whole of Kashmir belongs to India, but one-third is under Pakistan's occupation, and Pakistan has often violated the ceasefire line.

Many years have passed since then. A plebiscite could not be held because Pakistan would not withdraw her forces first. While Pakistan's forces remained, a plebiscite could not be free and fair. After nearly twenty years part of Kashmir is still under Pakistan's occupation. The Security Council has not been able to make Pakistan carry out its resolutions. The Council made more than one attempt to mediate, but it did not succeed. The Council now wants India and Pakistan to settle the question themselves directly. But Pakistan's leaders refuse. They go on talking of a plebiscite.

In September 1965, after Jawaharlal's death, Pakistan committed a second aggression in Kashmir. First she sent large batches of raiders across the ceasefire line, and then she also attacked across the Indian boundary in the south. India retaliated and attacked Pakistan. The Security Council intervened and brought about a ceasefire. It again said that the two countries should settle the dispute directly between themselves. The Soviet Union then took the initiative and called a conference of Indian and Pakistani leaders at Tashkent. They agreed not to use force in settling disputes, and to settle Kashmir and other disputes directly between themselves. But Pakistan has not observed the Tashkent Agreement. She refuses to agree to direct talks.

Pakistan always talks of her right to Kashmir, forgetting that she is the aggressor and has no such right. Her leaders think that Kashmir should belong to Pakistan merely because most of the people of Kashmir are Muslims. But India also has millions of Muslims, and she feels that merely because most of the people of Kashmir are Muslims, it need not belong to Pakistan. For nearly twenty years the Muslims of Kashmir have settled down to a life of peace along with the rest of India, and they do not want to be disturbed. Elections have been held in Kashmir several times, and the people have expressed their wishes in favour of staying as a part of the Indian Union, while Pakistan has not held direct elections even for her own people. It is only when Pakistan threatens to use force that the people of Kashmir are disturbed.

For India, there is no Kashmir problem. If there is a dispute with Pakistan over Kashmir, she is prepared to settle it directly and peacefully. Jawaharlal settled other disputes with Pakistan generously. He always worked for friendship with Pakistan. Pakistan had no better friend than him. He wanted peace in Kashmir and he worked for it till the end.

19   India and the World

Among Indians, Jawaharlal knew the most about the rest of the world. He had read history deeply, had travelled widely, and thought much about India's relations with other countries. Even in 1946, when he was only the vice-president of the Viceroy's Executive Council, he laid down what would be free India's policy towards the rest of the world. Jawaharlal was not only the head of the cabinet but a member for external affairs. He called the Asian Relations Conference, and it became a rallying point for the Asian people who were still fighting for their freedom. He also extended a hand of friendship to the people of Africa.

When India became free in 1947, Jawaharlal became both Prime Minister and Foreign Minister. He knew the most about foreign affairs, and so he remained Foreign Minister till his death. The world also liked his being his country's Foreign Minister. Whoever else might have been the Foreign Minister, Jawaharlal would have made the foreign policy.

He knew it best, for he had shaped India's foreign

policy when she was still a subject nation. Free India's foreign policy grew from subject India's foreign policy.

'Foreign policy' means a country's relations with the rest of the world. Jawaharlal had grown under Gandhi's influence, and he wanted to introduce truth, non-violence, and other ideas of Gandhi into the relations between countries. India wanted peace in the world and she worked for it. She worked against nations wasting money and energy on arms. She worked against the atom bomb and the hydrogen bomb. She opposed military blocs like NATO (the North Atlantic Treaty Organization) and the establishment of military bases in other people's territories. If there was to be peace, all countries should be free. The rule of one country over another country is called colonialism. India was opposed to it.

India was free. But Jawaharlal wanted other countries also to be free. There were many countries in Asia and Africa that were not free. India worked for their freedom. She helped Indonesia and other countries to be free. She took up the cause of Asian and African countries till they were all free. For this, she had to oppose and displease Britain, France, Holland and other European countries which had colonies and were colonial powers. Their vast possessions were called empires. Those empires are now gone. But they were coming back in another form, with European countries establishing a new hold on their former colonies. Jawaharlal led the fight against this new colonialism also.

India was always trying to work for other countries, and people praised Jawaharlal for this. He said that India's policy was in India's own interest. If other countries were free, it would make India's own freedom strong. If there were peace in the world, India too would enjoy peace; and she needed it so that she could work for a better life for her people. If there was war, India would be drawn into it, and her own peace would be disturbed.

There were two groups of countries in the world. They were called power blocs because they were led by powerful nations. There was danger of a war between them. One power bloc was led by America and the other by the Soviet Union. America and the Soviet Union were now the biggest powers in the world. They had different political and economic systems and their ways of life were different. They carried on propaganda against each other throughout the world. It was called the 'cold war', because they did not fight with weapons.

Jawaharlal disliked cold war too, because it could lead to a hot war and destroy the world. Even in the days of the interim government he had said that India would not join either the American bloc or the Soviet bloc. To join either bloc would lead to conflict with the other bloc and encourage the two blocs to come to a clash. India was friendly with both America and the Soviet Union and would not be aligned with either bloc.

This policy was called the policy of non-alignment. The name was given to India's whole policy, but it was only a part of the policy. It meant that India was independent. Slowly other countries also followed India's policy, and the bloc of independent powers helped peace.

America and the Soviet Union were for a time angry with India for not joining them, but first the Soviet Union understood it and then America too began to understand it. In the end they showed respect for India's policy. They felt that it helped peace. They were giving up the cold war and becoming friendly to each other.

Nehru with President Kennedy of the U.S.; with President de Gaulle of France; with Queen Elizabeth of England; at Tashkent in Uzbek dress; and with Sir Abubakar Balewa and Dr. Nnamdi Azikiwe of Nigeria

With President and Madame Tito of Yugoslavia

With President Nasser in Cairo

Receiving Dr. Erhard of Germany

India had to act jointly with other countries to serve peace. She was active in the United Nations where all countries, except a few, worked together. She supported peace and disarmament and, in order to keep the peace, sent her troops to places where there was trouble. She supported the freedom movements and gave aid for the development of backward countries.

India also worked with Asian and African countries for their common good. In 1954 there was a conference of these countries at Bandung in Indonesia. Jawaharlal was the moving spirit there. There was later a conference of non-aligned countries in Belgrade in Yugoslavia, and Jawaharlal was again the moving spirit. These conferences condemned colonialism, racialism, and armaments and helped peace.

Jawaharlal established close friendship with President Nasser of Egypt and Marshal Tito of Yugoslavia. These two and Jawaharlal were known as the leaders of non-alignment. In 1956, when Britain, France, and Israel attacked Egypt, Jawaharlal strongly condemned the attack and the Egyptians have never forgotten it. He worked tirelessly to stop atom bomb tests. At last there was a treaty to stop them and he was the first head of government to sign it.

As Prime Minister Jawaharlal visited many countries, and he was received everywhere with respect, admiration, and love. He visited America, the Soviet Union, China and other countries and impressed people everywhere with his charm, energy and friendliness. He was on good terms with many leaders of the world and was as much known among the people of other countries as he was in his own. They all liked him because he stood for peace and cooperation among the nations.

20   China

Jawaharlal respected China as a big country with six hundred million people and with an age-old civilization. When Japan attacked China before the Second World War, his sympathies were with China. India was under British rule and could do nothing to help China, but he sent a medical mission on behalf of the Congress as a token of India's sympathy. In September 1939, he visited China to see the people defending themselves against Japan. He had to return because war had broken out in Europe.

At the time when India became free, there was civil war in China. The Communists, under the leadership of Mao Tse-tung, were fighting against the Kuomintang, the ruling party, which was under the leadership of Chiang Kai-shek. Chiang and the people around him were corrupt and unpopular. His troops deserted him. The Communists got hold of the arms left by the Japanese and swept through the country. Peking, the capital of China, surrendered and the Communists established their rule.

Jawaharlal had sympathy for the new Chinese revolution and he was among the first to recognize the Communist regime. A vast change had taken place. China was now under a strong and confident regime and Jawaharlal wanted India and China to work closely together as friends.

India and China were both big countries and there had never been any fighting between them. Both had old civilizations of which their people were proud, and there had been cultural exchanges between them for many centuries. They had a common border which was as long as two thousand miles. India and China were close neighbours, and they must live as good neighbours. Peace between them was possible and it was necessary. Jawaharlal thought like this, and the Chinese leaders seemed to think so too.

In 1950 there were differences between the two countries over Tibet. Tibet had been a buffer State between India and China. It was not an independent country; it was an autonomous region of China. China was overlord, but Tibet had a certain amount of freedom. Then China wanted to send troops to Lhasa, the capital of Tibet. This seemed strange to India. India had no right to Tibet; she had some trade posts and trading interests there. But she said that Tibet was autonomous and should enjoy social and cultural freedom. After some talks the Chinese agreed, and the Dalai Lama, the ruler of Tibet, was recognized.

In 1954 there was a treaty between India and China on Tibet. It was a very friendly treaty. Tibet was to remain autonomous and certain Indian rights were recognized. The treaty also laid down some principles. The most important of them was that no country should interfere in the affairs of another country. These principles were called the Five Principles of Peace, and came to be known as *Panchsheel*. These principles were gradually affirmed by most countries of the world.

The relations between India and China were close. People from each country visited the other, and there were cultural delegations. Jawaharlal was received warmly in China in 1954, and Chou En-Lai, the Chinese Prime Minister, received a warm welcome in India more than once. The Chinese leaders said that China and India had to go their different ways but they could be friendly. The Chinese knew that India was an independent country and that she was not an agent of any other power.

In 1950 there was a big war in Korea. The North Koreans, supported by the Chinese, were fighting the South Koreans who were supported by the Americans. India worked hard to bring about a truce and the Chinese appreciated Jawaharlal's efforts for peace. There was trouble in Indo-China also, and India was again active in working for peace. China appreciated this too. It was India that helped Mr. Chou En-Lai to attend the Bandung Conference.

Everything seemed well between China and India but there were differences about the border between them. When the treaty on Tibet was signed in 1954, the Chinese did not raise any doubts about the existing border. But in their maps of China the Chinese showed large areas of Indian territory, and when Jawaharlal raised the matter with Chou En-Lai, he said that the maps were old and would be changed. But slowly the Chinese raised more and more doubts about the border and made occasional thrusts into Indian territory.

In 1959 there was a revolt in Tibet, because the Chinese were oppressing the people. The Dalai Lama fled to the Indian border and sought refuge. India could not refuse him, and when the Dalai Lama was received in India, the Chinese were angry. They began abusing Jawaharlal and raised disputes about the border. Jawaharlal was patient. He did not want a conflict

With the Dalai Lama

between India and China, for it would be a long conflict and bad for both.

In 1962 the Chinese advanced again into Indian territory and India had to defend herself. The Chinese used a large force and advanced deep into India. It was a big crisis for her. The people rose like one man in defense of their land. There was alarm that the Chinese were advancing so far but Jawaharlal remained firm.

The Chinese knew they could not advance too far. The Indian people had not been prepared to meet a large-scale attack but now they prepared to drive the Chinese back. So the Chinese troops withdrew. The leaders of five countries, Ghana, Indonesia, Ceylon (now Sri Lanka), Burma (now Myanmar) and Egypt, met together at Colombo, the capital of Ceylon, and made proposals for peace. India was prepared for peace and accepted the proposals. But China did not. The position has not changed. China continues to be hostile to India and now and then threatens to attack again.

Jawaharlal was disappointed with China. China had betrayed his trust. He had been aware that China would one day give trouble. But he worked to see that there would be no trouble and he hoped that peace between the two countries would not be disturbed. He was not afraid to fight but he knew that the best way to fight was to make the people united and strong. China had vast armies and weapons. India had to develop her strength if she was to defend herself. So he was busy making his country strong.

China had struck suddenly with superior forces. Yet she had to withdraw and has not dared to attack India again. Even in the midst of danger, Jawaharlal remained brave and confident. He did not give up non-alignment. He knew that the Soviet Union would not support China against India, and he was proved to be correct. When others were afraid, he remained firm.

21   Modern Temples

Jawaharlal thought that freedom from foreign rule was not enough. The people must be not only free but happy and prosperous. They must be strong so that they could not be attacked or conquered by other peoples. They must not depend on other countries forever. They must be socially equal, and they must have equality of opportunity. For all this, the people must plan.

Jawaharlal had believed in planning long before Independence. He thought it was not good to work without a plan. The standard of living in a vast country like India could not be raised without planning. He made the Congress establish a Planning Committee in 1938, and he became its chairman. But nothing much could be done under the British regime. To carry out his ideas he had to wait till India got her freedom.

The Planning Commission was set up in 1950. Jawaharlal was its chairman till his death. He helped in the making of the first three Plans. Each was a Five Year Plan, and each Plan raised the standard of living of the people.

People were helped to produce more in agriculture, to bring more land under cultivation, and to raise the yield per acre. In industries, India was a backward country. Under British rule, she had missed the Industrial Revolution. Big industries were established for the first time under the Plans. It was difficult to make progress at once. But the three Plans took India forward. Jawaharlal was busy preparing the fourth Five Year Plan when he died.

Jawaharlal persisted with planning when few had faith in it. The old Congress was thinking of the spinning wheel and of village industries, but Jawaharlal believed in making India a modern country, capable of living in a modern age. So he established big dams, steel plants, and science laboratories. He did not neglect the villages and village industries, but his approach was modern. He believed in science and wanted it to be applied to make life richer and better.

Jawaharlal was a socialist. Under socialism the people make goods for use, not for profit. For this, the people as a whole, and not a few persons, must own the means by which goods are produced and distributed. Jawaharlal did not want a few people to become rich at the expense of other people. In India, he said, there must be planning, and that planning could only be socialist planning. A vast country like India could not make progress quickly without it. Democracy was bound to succeed in India and socialism was also bound to come. He believed that socialism was modern. It made use of science. Each country can have only its own kind of socialism. India must have a socialism for Indian conditions.

Soon after Independence, landlordism was abolished. The peasants became the masters of the land on which they worked. This was the first step necessary to improve agriculture. The village had to be improved in other ways also. The village people were to be organized and helped to make their lives better. This was called Community Development.

If India is to be developed quickly into a happy, prosperous country, the government must play a big part. Private people do not have enough money to start big industries. They are not interested in starting them. Jawaharlal thought that India must first have big dams. Dams store water from big rivers for irrigation and other purposes; they also produce electricity. Only the government could build these dams. Among the dams built under the Plans are those at Bhakra Nangal in Punjab, Hirakud in Orissa, and Nagarjuna Sagar in Andhra Pradesh.

Steel was also very important for progress, and India produced little steel. There was only one steel plant, at Jamshedpur in Bihar, and the same was in private hands. So the government set up big steel plants, one at Bhilai in Madhya Pradesh with Soviet help, one at Durgapur in West Bengal with British help, and one at Rourkela in Orissa with German help. Fertilizer was necessary to make the earth fertile and give a better yield. A fertilizer factory was established at Sindri in Jharkhand (earlier in Bihar) which soon became a model for other fertilizer factories.

Jawaharlal called these huge plants and projects India's modern temples. People worshipped gods for salvation, but that did not help them. They had learnt that salvation lies in abolishing poverty, in producing more food, in improving health. For this, the people must produce more and more of everything. While, they required the help of other countries, they could not depend on other countries forever. They must ultimately depend on themselves to produce everything they needed.

Jawaharlal also wanted that whatever is produced must be distributed fairly among the people. The rich should not grow richer and the poor even more poor. For this, too, planning was necessary.

Jawaharlal taught the people how to plan, how they must save, how they must put their savings in development, and how they must work hard. He also wanted the people, that is, the peasants, the workers, young men and women and children to get benefits immediately. He wanted India to be changed rapidly from an ancient country to a modern country. He was an impatient man and he made a whole people impatient for change.

22   People's Rule

Jawaharlal looked a Caesar in his imperious moods, but he was not one and he did not like Caesars. "We want no Caesar," he said, when dictators were fashionable in Europe, and Hitler and Mussolini had many admirers. Long before Independence, Jawaharlal had been a democrat. Democracy means the rule of the people by the people. It has been shown to be the best form of government. But there could be no democracy without freedom; there had to be freedom first.

By freedom Jawaharlal meant freedom for the people. They must be free to shape their freedom as they liked. He was close to them. They belonged to different regions, practised different religions, and spoke different languages. There were the Pathans, the Rajasthanis, the Assamese, the Malayalees, and others. They were different from each other. Yet they were alike. They had different backgrounds, different literatures, and different ways of living, but in essence their culture was one. There was something Indian underneath it all.

Jawaharlal liked this richness of Indian culture and

he wanted it to remain so. It made Indian democracy colourful, varied and vigorous. He thought of the people as millions and millions of individuals, each master of his fate. They had to work together, and unitedly make India happy and prosperous. This was democracy.

Jawaharlal was a great leader of the people. He understood them well. He knew how to talk to them and inspire them. They admired him as a brave, thoughtful, and adventurous man. They had great faith that he would lead them to a great future. He had vast power and he enjoyed that power because it helped him to do things. But he did not want to force people to do anything. He was a leader who led people by persuasion. He liked to discuss problems with others and take decisions in consultation. He was a democrat by faith.

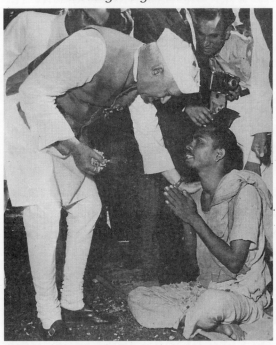

The Prime Minister listening to a villager's grievances

The Constituent Assembly had been his idea. He thought it was the people's represen-tatives who should decide how the people would govern themselves. The people were the masters and they had to decide their future. With freedom came democracy. Every man or woman had the right to vote. Many people did not know how to read or write, but Jawaharlal

97

felt that everyone of a prescribed age should take part in electing their representatives. It was by working together that they could feel that they were a nation. Jawaharlal under-stood that India was changing, with her roots in the past. There must be change but it should not be imposed. There should be no majority culture or minority culture, no Hindu culture or Muslim culture. It should be Indian culture.

In a democracy people decide matters by discussion, not by force. Jawaharlal was a great democrat because he had a great capacity for discussion. He spoke in a simple, persuasive way. In Parliament, too, he believed in discussion. He was the greatest parliamentarian of his time. He always showed respect for Parliament; he was always courteous to those who did not agree with him; and he was ready to admit mistakes. He was sometimes grave and sometimes gay. He was regular and punctual, and people liked not only what he said but the way he said it.

Democracy, he once said, demands many virtues. It demands ability. It demands dedication to work. It demands cooperation and discipline. He claimed that democracy had worked successfully in India. He did not claim the credit for himself; he gave all the credit to the people. In four general elections the people had showed that they could vote intelligently and peacefully. There were so many of them and most of them were illiterate, but they took a keen interest in the elections. It was a huge operation but they carried it out with success. Everyone said that the elections were free and fair. They were the largest elections held anywhere in the world.

Democracy at the top was not enough. Jawaharlal wanted democracy from the bottom. He wanted people's councils at the village level also. In State after State they were introduced and they have been working well. The working of democracy has not been perfect. But people learn by experience and correct their mistakes. Jawaharlal believed that democracy alone could correct its mistakes. There were many who felt uncertain about what would happen after him. But he had faith in the people and that faith has been justified.

23 Prime Minister

To be the Prime Minister of a vast country like India is a hard and difficult job, and Jawaharlal was Prime Minister for seventeen long years. He worked long hours, till late at night and sometimes till the early hours of the morning. He sometimes took time off to relax, but he had no real rest. He told the people again and again that they were sentenced to hard labour. They had to work hard to build the country. "*Aram haram hai!* (Rest is not proper)," he often said.

Jawaharlal was not merely Prime Minister. He was the leader of the nation. He was the life and soul of the Congress. He represented his country to the rest of the world. India meant Jawaharlal and Jawaharlal meant India. He was the head of the government, and he took a great interest in every part of the work. For some time he was both Prime Minister and Congress President. He gave ideas to the Congress and the Congress laid down the programmes for the government. He met distinguished visitors from abroad and had to hold important talks with them. He had to entertain them too.

He had also to pay visits to many countries to strengthen friendship between them and India and to maintain peaceful relations. He addressed the United Nations once in Paris and twice in New York. There he called upon the leaders of the world to disarm and seek peace.

Jawaharlal had to attend Parliament regularly and address the House on important occasions. He presided over meetings of the cabinet and took an active interest in the work of every ministry. He wrote notes of advice to Chief Ministers and sent instructions to India's ambassadors. He presided over meetings of the Planning Commission and of the National Development Council. He inaugurated many projects all over the country and helped many people by attending functions arranged by them. He addressed sessions of the Congress. All over the country he spoke to large gatherings of people, asking them to love their country, to be united, and to work hard. He liked to move

Enjoying a joke with Dr. Albert Einstein, the famous scientist

With George Bernard Shaw

101

Addressing the General Assembly of the United Nations in New York

At a mass meeting in Ahmadnagar

among the people and learn about their needs. Whenever he met them he felt fresh and strong.

In 1962 Jawaharlal fell ill for the first time. But he recovered soon and was well again. In Parliament, he was still the best speaker. He was as quick as ever in his answers. At the time of the Chinese attack, he felt disappointed, but he stood firm as a rock. Some people panicked and wanted him to change his policies. He refused. He would not join either bloc and the leading countries of both blocs supported India.

Jawaharlal, with all his energy and good health for so many years, could work so hard because he felt he must work. He once said, "Gandhiji has put this ideal before us, that we should wipe out every tear from every eye. I do not think we can follow this ideal completely, but we must try to alleviate pain." He tried his best again and again. Yet there was so much to do. In his last years, he wrote on his writing pad the following lines from a poem by the American poet, Robert Frost:

> The woods are lovely, dark and deep,
> But I have promises to keep.
> And miles to go before I sleep,
> And miles to go before I sleep.

He kept these lines in mind till the last hours of his life.

24   Chacha

Jawaharlal was a rare human being. He did not think of himself as a leader or as Prime Minister. He was always his usual self and treated all people, young and old, with consideration. He was sometimes lost in thought and would be in different moods. He was upset by untruthfulness, sloth, or inefficiency, but he would soon be his usual self again. He always behaved with dignity and grace. He did not know what it was to be mean. He met hundreds of people, and everyone of them remembered some act of kindness of his. He would help old women, he would play with children, he would enquire of a peasant how he was getting on, and he would quietly help someone with money. Foreigners who met him were charmed by him.

Jawaharlal did not care what happened to him or to his reputation after he was gone.

If people chose to think of him, then, he said, he would like them to say, "This was a man who, with all his mind and heart, loved India and the Indian people. And they in turn were indulgent to him and gave him of their love abundantly and extravagantly."

Jawaharlal woke up at dawn and did some exercises before getting ready for the day. Breakfast was his favourite meal. He would help himself to porridge and he would cut fruit delicately and gracefully and

Playing with a tiger cub

Happy in the company of children

distribute pieces to his guests. He would tell delightful stories. He would then go down to meet the crowd of visitors who went daily to see him. Then he would go to see his pets, either tiger cubs or pandas. He went to his office punctually. There he kept his secretaries and stenographers busy. There would be interviews with officials, foreign visitors, or other people. His lunch was light, sometimes Indian and sometimes European. He would relax a little and go back to the office and work again.

In the evening he would do all kinds of things, address a meeting, hold talks with visitors, or see a dance performance. Dinner would again be a relaxed affair. He often had guests for breakfast, lunch, or dinner and according to need, he would talk or relax or be lost in thought. He was a good host. Sometimes he gave a lunch in his garden, and then he would take his guests to see the pandas.

Jawaharlal kept his word. If he said he would be present somewhere at a certain time, he would be there. He was never late. He hated slovenliness and unpunctuality. He lost his temper if something went wrong, but he would soon be calm and forgiving. He was a good correspondent. He answered every letter he received, though he had to dictate many notes and write so much. Even when he dictated, his style was easy, clear, and faultless. He put his trust in people. Some of them let him down. But he believed a person was good, unless it was proved he was not.

To children he gave much. He liked to talk to them, to throw his garlands to them, and to play with them. Though he was a busy man, he found time to attend children's functions. He was known to them as Chacha (Uncle) Nehru and on his birthday, November 14, he met thousands of them at a rally. He saw in children the future generations, and he knew that the future of the country depended on them. His fondness for children increased with years. Many children who met him and received prizes from him remember him with love and reverence. He loved animals and birds, too. He was in tune with nature, and he loved to watch its changing scenery. He often went to the hills and the woods, to be away from the world of men, but he came back to that world to lead people in their struggle again.

Jawaharlal was a great man who did great things, but many people remember him as a great man who was very human in everything he did.

25   Last Days

Jawaharlal had high ambitions for his country. He was proud of his people and of their capacity to carry on, as they had carried on for centuries, with hope and courage. He wanted to work for them till the end. He did not care what happened to him. Even when he was ill, he thought of nothing but working for his country.

He once said, "There is one ambition left in me that in the few years left to me I should throw myself, with all the strength and energy left in me, into the work of building up India. I want to do it to the uttermost, till I am exhausted and thrown away as on the scrap-heap. I am not interested in what you or anybody thinks of me afterwards. It is enough for me that I have exhausted myself, my strength and energy, in India's task."

He was always a man of promise. When he was sixty, the Five Year Plans were yet to come. At seventy, he was full of thoughts for the future of India. He was sometimes very tired and twice he wanted to resign from Prime Ministership, in 1954 and in 1958, so that he could get fresh again. But both times he was persuaded not to resign. He did not want to retire for rest. There could be no rest for him whether in office or out of it. India's problems weighed heavily on him and he had a responsibility to his people, whether he was Prime Minister or not. So he went on working, even after his first illness in 1962.

Jawaharlal was more energetic and adventurous than younger men, and he took an interest in everything. He went to Bhubaneswar in Orissa (now Odisha) in January 1963 to attend a session of the All-India Congress Committee. There he had a mild stroke. His left side was slightly paralyzed. Still he worked on.

When he returned to Delhi he tried to take some rest, but he could not rest for long. He flew to the border between India and Nepal where he laid the foundation stone of a big irrigation project. He attended Parliament regularly and addressed the House. He presided over a meeting of the Planning Commission to give shape to the Fourth Five Year Plan. There was a session of the All-India Congress Committee in Bombay. He surprised everyone by taking a great interest in its proceedings and making vigorous speeches.

At a press conference in Delhi someone asked him, "After Nehru, who?"

He answered, "My lifetime is not going to end soon": He hoped he would live to work more, and the people had even greater hope.

Jawaharlal, however, needed rest, and in May 1964 he flew to Dehra Dun in a helicopter for a short holiday. There he looked through several files. He read and he wrote. He met old friends. He was looking relaxed and cheerful. On May 26 he returned to Delhi. He worked till midnight. In the morning, on May 27, he woke up feeling uneasy and he began to read a book. His attendant asked him how he felt. He said he was not feeling too well. He lay in bed and felt too ill to get up. Doctors came, and they did their best. Indira was by his side. She offered her blood, if needed, so that his life could be saved. But it was of no use.

The news of Jawaharlal's illness spread throughout the country. There was hope that he might recover. The people had been accustomed to his presence and refused to think that he would die. At 2 p.m. the attempt to save him had to be given up. He was dead.

The nation was grief-stricken. Parliament was meeting at that time, the news was announced, and it was adjourned. The whole world was bereaved. Messages from leaders from all over the world came pouring in. The nation was in mourning. On the morning of May 28, Jawaharlal was cremated with State honours. The representatives of many governments came from distant countries and were present at the funeral.

Some days later, Jawaharlal's last will and testament was published. In it, he said:

"I am proud of that great inheritance that has been, and is, ours, and am conscious that I too, like all of us, am a link in the unbroken chain which goes back to the dawn of history in the immemorial past of India. That chain I would not break, for I treasure it and seek inspiration from it. And as witness of this desire of my mind and as my last homage to India's cultural inheritance, I am making this request that a handful of my ashes be thrown into the Ganga at Allahabad to be carried to the great ocean that washes India's shores.

"The major portion of my ashes should, however, be disposed of otherwise. I want these to be carried high up into the air in an aeroplane and scattered from that height over the fields where the peasants of India toil, so that they might mingle with the dust and soil of India and become an indistinguishable part of India."

Jawaharlal's ashes were thrown into the Ganga and scattered from the air. But that was not the end of him. He lives in the minds and hearts of people not only in India but elsewhere. The Jawahar Jyoti goes on burning in Teen Murti, the house where he lived and worked for so many years. Thousands of people go to Shanti Vana, where he was cremated, to pay their homage.

Jawaharlal needs no memorial. The whole of modern India is a memorial to him. The story of his life will be told and retold. It is the story of a brave, hardworking, and chivalrous man, who loved his people with all his mind and heart, who worked for them till the end of his life, and who built a hopeful future for them. They cannot forget him. And they know they must carry on his work.

The house where Jawaharlal lived for
17 years—now the Nehru Museum